AI for Emotional Well-being

Tools and Resources for Mental Health Support

Table of Contents

Chapter 1. Introduction

Emotional well-being is beyond just feeling positive; it's a holistic experience of contentment, happiness and a state of seeming harmony with self and surroundings. It is about revitalizing the mind, celebrating the spirit, and nurturing the sole essence - our emotions. This Special Report shines the spotlight on an unparalleled support mechanism for our emotional well-being - Artificial Intelligence (AI). Not so daunting or chilly as it may sound, AI is increasingly becoming a warm companion in our journey towards achieving mental health and emotional well-being. This report illustrates how AI, a sophisticated technology, is offering simple, immediate, and efficient tools and resources to augment your journey toward emotional stability. It's an insightful and reassuring dive into the world of AI for mental health support, promising to leave you informed and inspired. So, wrap yourself in your favorite blanket, grab a warm cup of coffee, and embark on a soothing voyage of discovery – all about you, AI, and your emotional well-being. Let this intriguing synthesis of technology and tranquility give you reasons to associate AI not just with intellect, but with emotional intelligence too!

Chapter 2. Unveiling AI: More than Just Code

Artificial Intelligence, often assigned to the realm of 1s and 0s, may seem at first to operate in a sphere far removed from the raw, ephemeral, and often nuanced world of emotions. As a term, 'artificial intelligence' carries with it stereotypes of cold, emotionless computation and logic devoid of empathy. Yet, on a deeper dive, we discover this potent form of technology can offer something more profound - it can give us tools to better navigate our emotional landscape.

2.1. AI and Emotional Intelligence: An Unlikely Union?

Emotional intelligence refers to the ability to identify, understand, use, and manage emotions in positive ways to relieve stress, communicate effectively, empathize with others, overcome challenges, and defuse conflicts. It is an essential aspect of overall mental health and well-being. On the surface, associating artificial intelligence, a computing technology, with emotional intelligence, a deeply human attribute, might seem paradoxical. But as we start to unravel the complex tapestry of AI, this seeming paradox unravels as well.

AI, at its core, is a tool - a product of human ingenuity designed to solve problems and create efficiencies. Its form and function are essentially shaped by its purpose, guided by the needs and issues it seeks to address. When applied to the arena of emotional well-being, AI can be fashioned in such a way to address challenges people face on their journey towards achieving better mental health. With Machine Learning, natural language processing, and other advanced capabilities, AI can be trained to recognize and understand human emotions, and even respond in ways that assist in managing emotional well-being.

2.2. The Role of Machine Learning in Emotional Support

Machine learning is a subset of AI that provides machines the ability to learn and improve from experience without being explicitly programmed. In the context of mental health, it is through machine learning that AI gets the ability to "understand" human emotions. It does so by examining patterns in data - for example, the words people use, the tone of their voice, or even patterns in clicking behavior when interacting with a digital tool. It pinpoints certain emotional states based on these patterns and makes probable predictions.

It is worth noting the profound difference between a machine's understanding of emotions and a human's. While humans perceive emotions through an amalgamation of lived experiences, memories, and feelings, a machine's understanding is purely based on the data and patterns it's been trained on. Nevertheless, this data-driven approach can be surprisingly effective in certain instances, such as in identifying emotions from text or helping people better understand their emotional states.

2.3. Bridging the Gap: Natural Language Processing

Another formidable weapon in AI's arsenal is Natural Language Processing (NLP) - a technology that enables machines to understand human language in a valuable way. It lies at the intersection of computer science, artificial intelligence, and computational linguistics.

NLP allows for a more natural interaction between humans and machines, through the spoken or written word. In the context of mental health, this can mean delivering therapy via chat or voice interface - removing barriers to entry, offering anonymous support, and providing help at any time of the day or night. AI can provide reliable, non-judgmental assistance, capable of respecting user's privacy by offering screening or support while maintaining confidentiality.

2.4. Emotional AI: Reading Between The Lines

AI technology, which analyzes emotions, is known as Emotion AI or Affective Computing. It involves the study and development of systems and devices that can recognize, interpret, process, and simulate human affects - a spectrum of emotions and moods. By observing verbal and non-verbal cues, AI algorithms can help to identify human moods, offering a kind of emotional radar.

Applications of Emotion AI in the mental health space are significant. From AI-driven mobile applications that regularly track a user's emotional state and provide stress reduction techniques to AI chatbots trained to offer psychological support in times of crisis, Emotion AI can play a pivotal part in individual journeys towards emotional well-being.

2.5. AI's Impact on Mental Health Services

AI's unique advantage is its scalability, which critical in addressing growing challenges in mental health care. With AI-powered mental health tools, individuals can access immediate help at any time, from the comfort of their homes. Such tools also have the potential to provide resources for those who might otherwise be unable to access mental health services due to issues of cost, distance, or even the stigma associated with seeking such help.

Moreover, AI systems can be a companion to traditional therapeutic methods, providing actionable insights to therapists. By analyzing session transcripts and detecting patterns, these systems can assist therapists in understanding their clients' issues better and guiding them effectively towards their healing journey.

In conclusion, this marriage of technology and emotion reveals AI to be more than just lines of code. It's a sophisticated suite of tools that, when keenly shaped and carefully applied, can offer transformative solutions to nurture our emotional health. As we welcome AI into our lives, let us look beyond its technical magnificence, recognizing its potential as a supportive ally in our pursuit of emotional well-being.

Chapter 3. Mapping Emotions: The Interplay of AI and Emotional Quotient

The journey to understand how AI can bolster our emotional well-being begins with understanding emotions themselves and how they're being mapped digitally. It's the mating dance of the rational and the emotional – an intricate ballet where technology meets the human soul.

3.1. The Complexity of Emotions

The human emotional framework is complex, multifaceted, and largely subjective. Emotions are interwoven in our DNA and are pivotal to our very existence. On the surface, feelings may manifest as happiness, sadness, anger, fear, surprise, or disgust. But delve deeper and you'll encounter an intricate network, a rich tapestry of feelings - from despair to delight, from rejection to recognition. Being able to identify, decode, and address the whole spectrum of these emotions is the first step towards achieving emotional well-being.

3.2. AI and Emotion Recognition

With its innate ability to analyze and map patterns, AI has extended its reach into emotion recognition. Large datasets, machine learning (ML), and natural language processing (NLP) have made it possible for AI to accurately measure human affect. Advanced algorithms are now capable of processing vast information, distinguishing subtle emotional signals, tones, facial expressions, and even physiological data. This has made AI an increasingly reliable technology for pinpointing our emotional states and, importantly, predicting our emotional needs.

3.3. Emotional Quotient and AI

Emotional Quotient (EQ), also known as Emotional Intelligence, is the ability to identify, understand, and manage our own emotions and the emotions of others. Widely accepted as equal, if not more important than IQ, EQ facilitates interpersonal relationships, reduces anxiety, and promotes self-awareness. By extending AI capabilities towards understanding and managing the EQ, we take a giant leap in harnessing technology for emotional well-being.

While it's true that AI cannot 'feel' emotions as humans do, it's increasingly becoming proficient at mimicking emotional comprehension. AI can process and analyze data to yield insights about individuals' emotional states, offering therapeutic interventions and suggesting self-help measures. AI can also anticipate emotional changes based on patterns and behaviors, helping individuals to manage emotional fluctuations.

3.4. Mapping Emotions with AI

Equipped with sentiment analysis and predictive abilities, AI is quickly becoming a tool for individuals seeking emotional well-being. Of course, the algorithmic interpretation of emotion is not without its challenges. Emotions are abstruse, contextual, and innately human. The high degree of human emotion variability can prove to be a challenging labyrinth for AI to navigate.

Despite these complexities, AI has taken significant strides in emotion mapping, in part owing to its ability to process large volumes of data and uncover patterns. From assessing tone of voice and interpreting facial expressions to examining physiological reactions, AI tools are being built to map our emotional journeys. Advanced analytics and ML help understand emotional responses, varying stress levels, and psychological insights, thereby helping individuals keep a check on their emotional health.

3.5. Emotional Chatbots

One of the recent developments in AI assisting emotional well-being is emotional chatbots. These AI applications use ML algorithms to analyze text for emotional content. They then respond with empathetic replies, creating an engaging, human-like conversation. Emotional chatbots can provide mood-based recommendations, such as music, books, or mindfulness exercises, contributing actively to the user's emotional well-being.

3.6. Ethical Considerations and Limitations

While AI's role in mapping emotions sounds promising, it's equally important to consider its limitations and ethical considerations. Handling sensitive emotional data warrants the utmost care around privacy and ethics. Decisions made based on AI analysis must be made responsibly, considering its potential for misuse. It's also crucial to remember that AI is merely a tool, and cannot replace the nuanced intuition and empathy of human therapists and specialists.

In conclusion, AI holds immense potential to foster emotional intelligence, offering an intriguing blend of technology and tranquility. As we continue to explore and combat the complexities of human emotions, AI stands as an unflinching ally, digitizing and mapping emotions like never before. The journey towards understanding our emotions better just got a lot more interesting, with a dash of AI charm!

Chapter 4. Tapping into AI for Stress Management

Humans have, for centuries, been trying to master stress management. In today's fast-paced world, it's more crucial than ever. Artificial Intelligence (AI) is at the forefront of helping us understand, manage, and alleviate stress. This steadfast digital companion is evolving into an important player in the realm of mental health by offering unique tools and techniques that adapt to the needs of the individual, promoting healthier and more balanced mental lives.

4.1. AI: Discerning Stress Patterns

For an algorithm to help in managing stress, it first has to recognize stress. This is where AI shines. Powerful and sophisticated machine learning algorithms – subsets of AI, work by observing, understanding, and learning human stress patterns. These patterns may be recognized through physiological metrics (like heart rate or skin conductance), speech characteristics, facial expressions, or even sleep patterns.

Many wearable technologies nowadays comprise sensors that monitor heart rate, skin temperature, or movement. These physiological data readings may indicate stress levels when processed through AI algorithms. For example, elevated heart rates when not associated with physical activity can indicate emotional distress.

AI can also identify stress factors from user-generated data such as messages, social media use, and browsing patterns. This data, when processed through natural language processing (NLP), a subfield of AI, can provide insights into an individual's mental state, mood, and stress level. Although this technological account of people's mental state may not be perfect, it offers the substantial power of early stress detection which is a crucial step in effective stress management.

4.2. AI Fostering Self Awareness

Self-awareness is a key attribute in managing stress effectively. AI technology can foster self-awareness by providing real-time feedback on our noticeable and unnoticeable habits which may contribute to stress. Smart apps can detect patterns in sleep, physical activity, diet, and even social interactions – all crucial to emotional well-being.

Large amounts of data can be processed swiftly by AI to give us a clearer picture of our stress landscape and identify potential stress triggers. With this information, we can make adjustments to our lifestyle, behavior, and mindset that may help reduce stress.

AI can also help in the development of mindfulness, a state wherein we focus our attention on the present. Several AI-based mobile applications deliver personalized mindfulness and meditation exercises, which aid in stress relief based on our observed habits and preferences.

4.3. Personalized AI-based Interventions

Artificial intelligence is revolutionizing stress management by not only identifying stress but offering personalized methods to manage it. These interventions are tailored according to the individual's specific needs and preferences. This personalization based on data is what sets AI apart from traditional stress management techniques.

For instance, some AI applications use cognitive-behavioral therapy (CBT) strategies, manipulating them to match individual user data, providing a customized approach to manage stress. Such programs can help individuals shift problematic thought patterns and develop more effective stress coping strategies on their own.

Besides CBT, AI tools also support biofeedback techniques, mindfulness practices, and other relaxation exercises that are nimble and user-specific.

4.4. AI for In-The-Moment Stress Support

AI, applied to mental health, is dynamic. Emerging technologies allow for immediate help, wherever and whenever it is required. Stress can surface at any time, and managing it takes precedence whenever it does. This is where AI can sometimes prove superior than a human supporter; an AI-based tool or app is available round the clock, ready to provide support as needed with little to no wait time.

Moreover, AI can offer in-the-moment advice based on real-time data. Many AI-powered tools offer swift, personalized coping strategies following stressful situations. From recommending a quick mindfulness exercise after detecting elevated stress to providing soothing music based on your personal preference, AI is continuously working in the background to make stress management as seamless and immediate as possible.

4.5. The Future of AI in Stress Management

The future of AI in stress management is bright, promising a convergence of advanced technologies with user-friendly interfaces with the potential to revolutionize mental health care. We might see AI technology becoming more ubiquitous, with deeper integration into our lifestyles and routines. The focus is likely to shift from mere stress identification to prevention and prediction, with AI providing proactive stress management strategies tailored to our personal patterns and predispositions.

As AI in tandem with mental wellness grows in leaps and bounds, privacy will be a critical aspect requiring constant vigilance. Conversations on safeguarding personal data and consent for data sharing will shape AI usage patterns, thereby influencing its adoption rates.

In conclusion, Artificial Intelligence, often perceived as cerebral and distant, has started to engage with the realm of emotions – understanding, responding, and even predicting them. It's playing a vital role in assisting individuals in navigating through their journey toward mental and emotional well-being. Our path to achieving effective stress management now includes an unexpected yet warmly welcomed collaborator – AI. Its nuanced understanding of stress as a variable, non-linear, and unique human experience is helping develop revolutionary stress management models in the form of personalized, accessible, and immediate support systems. Truly, the relationship between humans and AI is not just about intellect but more so about emotional intelligence. AI is no longer just a technical tool; it's a compassionate companion in the pursuit of a tranquil life.

Chapter 5. The Role of AI in Enhancing Positive Thinking

Positive thinking is a mental and emotional attitude focusing on the bright side of life and expecting positive outcomes. One can enhance it by engaging in practices such as mindfulness, meditation, and cognitive behavioral therapy. However, the incorporation of Artificial Intelligence (AI) has brought an unprecedented level of support in enhancing positive thinking. From AI-based chatbots for CBT to AI-driven meditation apps, AI applications in mental health applications are increasing. This part of the report will delve into the role AI plays in promoting positive thinking, its mechanism, and its impact in detail.

5.1. AI in Daily Life: Destigmatizing Mental Health

With a vast majority of people using smartphones, AI has wedged into our daily lives, counseling us toward positive thinking, and helping to break down the stigma around mental health. AI-powered applications and gadgets are now readily available, providing simple, quick and effective mindfulness practices, mood tracking, and therapy sessions just a click away. These applications, designed keeping human psyche and experiences into account, aid users in dealing with anxiety, stress, depression, and other emotional challenges.

AI-based virtual companions or chatbots are programmed to offer Cognitive Behavioral Therapy (CBT). Traditional CBT involves working with a therapist to identify negative thought patterns and substitute them with positive ones. AI chatbots like Woebot and Wysa can support this process, interacting with users in an empathetic and compassionate manner while remaining available 24/7, imitating the comfort of a friendly chat yet offering scientifically-proven therapeutic techniques.

5.2. Algorithm of Positivity: AI Learning and Adapting

Behind the AI applications fostering positive thinking is complex algorithms, machine learning, and neural network structures. AI learns from the data provided and gradually adapts to the individual user's needs. Most AI-powered mental health apps incorporate algorithms designed to identify patterns or fluctuations in an individual's moods, thoughts, and behaviors. Machine learning algorithms meticulously analyze user data over time and provide personalized feedback, recommendations, and interventions.

An example is the AI chatbot, Replika, which develops a unique personality based on user interactions, evolving into a virtual companion. Leveraging AI's text mining and Natural Language Processing (NLP) capabilities, these chatbots can analyze text inputs to understand user's emotional states and respond appositely to induce positivity. The ultimate goal is to tailor the approach to suit individual needs better and promote positivity proactively.

5.3. Quantifying Emotion: AI in Emotional Analytics

Although emotions are abstract and qualitative, AI has the potential to quantify them. By leveraging emotional analytics, AI applications such as Moodfit and MoodMission identify patterns in factors affecting users' moods. By suggesting activities to uplift mood and recommending changes mental health practices, they aid users in curating a personalized roadmap to positivity.

Moreover, various AI applications use sentiment analysis to identify and extract subjective information from their users —favoring the development of strategies to counter negative thoughts and foster positivity.

5.4. Pervasive Positivity: AI for Everyone

AI-enabled mental health programs aren't just for those undergoing treatments or mental health conditions. They are for anyone seeking to induce positivity in their lives, perhaps looking to manage their stresses better or seeking to improve their overall emotional wellbeing. Tools such as Headspace leverage AI to provide tailored meditation and stress-management techniques.

In the corporate world, AI-based systems are being implemented to assess employees' mental health and offer solutions. Implementing AI can lead to proactive mental health management, offering avenues to foster positive thinking, and affecting productivity positively.

AI's role in enhancing positive thinking is multi-faceted. It presents an avenue of all-inclusive, non-judgmental, and unbiased assistance that is not confined by time or space. Through continual learning and adaptation, AI tools provide constructive and personalized strategies to foster positivity, bringing a unique blend of technology and positivity at our fingertips. Balancing the equations of human emotions, AI silhouettes as a promising beacon of positivity and improved mental health in the modern world.

Chapter 6. AI Chatbots: Your 24/7 Mental Health Companion

In today's fast-paced world, instant help, support, or information is only as far away as your nearest digital device. Among the many applications of Artificial Intelligence (AI), one significant implementation lies in the realm of mental health, and it is being powerfully embodied in AI chatbots. These AI-powered chatbots are offering support, information, and resources - 24/7. Their presence is unobtrusive yet reliable, making them an ideal tool for the journey toward emotional well-being. Let's delve into the world of AI chatbots and explore how you can leverage their capabilities in your pursuit of mental health.

6.1. Understanding AI Chatbots

So, what exactly are AI chatbots? Quite simply, they are software tools that use artificial intelligence to communicate with humans in natural language. They do so through text or voice interactive methods, making use of machine learning algorithms to understand and respond to users' questions and conversations. Typically, AI chatbots learn over time, improving the relevance and accuracy of their responses based on information gathered from past conversations.

An advantage of AI chatbots in mental health support is their availability. When humans are unavailable or inconvenient, a chatbot offers a patient, private and non-threatening interface to express feelings or difficulties. Moreover, the absence of stigmatization and judgment encourages those reluctant to seek face-to-face assistance.

6.2. AI Chatbots at Work

AI chatbots help users in managing their mental health by employing different techniques. They're designed to help with a range of issues, from stress and anxiety to depression.

For example, mindfulness is an emerging focus within the mental health sphere. AI chatbots can guide you through mindfulness exercises that help reduce stress levels, promote relaxation and improve sleep quality. The chatbot can prompt you to slow your breathing or lead you through a calming visualization exercise, supporting self-guided practices at your convenience.

Likewise, some AI chatbots are equipped to use Cognitive Behavioral Therapy (CBT) methodologies, a common type of psychotherapy that teaches users to reframe negative thinking patterns and behaviors. A chatbot employing CBT technique can help you understand and change thought patterns leading to harmful behaviors or distressing feelings.

6.3. Reliability of Chatbots

The question arises: how reliable are AI chatbots? Can they replace human therapists? Short answer: no, they cannot replace humans. Nevertheless, they have proven to contribute significantly to mental health care. A well-programmed AI chatbot can provide a standard care level, identifying users' mood changes over time, tracking wellness, and even sending alerts if a user's condition seems to worsen. However, they are more of an adjunct to human-delivered care, a companion rather than a substitute.

6.4. The Role of Privacy and Ethics

A sensitive area when dealing with AI chatbots for mental health is privacy and data ethics. Your interactions with an AI chatbot should remain confidential and inaccessible to unauthorized personnel. Strong data encryption protocols, adherence to privacy, and ethics standards are integral to a reliable AI chatbot. It's crucial only to engage with platforms with a clear confidentiality policy and a solid reputation.

6.5. Road Ahead: Future Trends

AI technologies are, of course, seeing continuous development. Emotion AI is a field aiming to improve machine detection and interpretation of human emotional signals. This will enable chatbots to recognize your emotional state from your text or voice tone. Plus, more sophisticated sentiment analysis will improve the chatbot's ability to respond appropriately to your mental and emotional state.

To sum up, the role of AI chatbots in mental health support is promising. The 24/7 availability, privacy, and personalized responsive systems they offer can augment traditional therapy methods and self-care measures. But remember that while AI chatbots are valuable tools, they should not supplant human healthcare providers. Mental health is a complex and nuanced field best navigated with both human empathy and the assistance of AI technologies.

Chapter 7. Online Therapy: How AI is Decoding the Future

While the dawn of modern technology has initiated a series of rapid developments, their integration into healthcare, particularly mental healthcare, has opened new doors to holistic well-being. Online therapy, supported by artificial intelligence (AI), is paving newer and more accessible paths toward therapy, bringing the future into the present along with our emotional and mental care.

7.1. Unveiling the Concept: Online Therapy Supported by AI

Imagine being able to share your mental health concerns and access therapy anytime, from anywhere. A concept once restricted to the realms of science fiction is gradually materializing into reality, thanks to the collaborative efforts of innovators, mental health experts, and AI technologies. AI-powered online therapy integrates the sophistication of AI technology with the personal experience of therapy to provide advanced therapeutic assistance.

By emulating human-like communicational abilities, AI is striving to create an environment where the user feels heard, understood, and supported. The underlying algorithms are designed to recognize emotional cues, respond empathetically, and suggest tailored coping mechanisms based on individual concerns.

Online therapy houses a robust database of mental health-related insights, therapeutic interventions, and stress management techniques, providing the AI with ample resources to make reliable suggestions. Drawn from worldwide recognized practices, this knowledge base assists in establishing a therapy module for each user, delivering personal therapy at your fingertips.

7.2. The Benefits: Efficiency and Accessibility

AI-assisted online therapy brings along a bouquet of benefits that have the potential to revolutionize mental healthcare. Beyond just being a convenient alternative to traditional, in-person therapy, AI extends the richness of professional therapeutic assistance along with the comfort of access at any point.

By breaking geographic boundaries and time constraints, the reach of therapy broadens, helping those who are remote, homebound, or unable to meet a therapist due to personal reasons. The interconnected digital world allows AI therapy to bring mental health support to your comfort zone, regardless of where you are.

Moreover, AI's efficiency lies in its immediate response. Unfettered by scheduling clashes or therapist availability, AI tools can engage in immediate conversations, providing support when you need it most. Postponing therapy due to logistical reasons often exacerbates stress, a hurdle that AI effortlessly resolves.

7.3. The Mechanics: AI Working Behind the Scenes

The sophistication of AI illuminates when it springs into action. It all begins when you initiate the conversation. The AI relies on your inputs to understand your state of mind and associated concerns. By engaging with you through text or voice, the AI platform gauges your emotional nuances and derives meaningful patterns.

The vast knowledge at AI's disposal empowers it to make suitable suggestions and offer effective coping strategies. Its goal is not just to respond correctly but to create a comfortable and understanding environment. Therefore, AI incorporates empathy in its responses, making it more than just an algorithm in action.

Every conversation you have with the AI tool is a learning experience for the algorithm which gradually fine-tunes its responses to your needs. With more interaction, AI becomes an increasingly reliable companion, ready to lend an understanding ear and extend psychological support tailored to you.

7.4. Implementation Examples: AI Therapeutic Platforms

A number of companies have developed AI-based platforms to offer therapeutic assistance. Woebot by Woebot Labs is an AI therapist that uses Cognitive Behavioural Therapy (CBT) foundations to offer mental health support. Users interact with Woebot through a messaging platform, where Woebot facilitates conversations, crafts responses based on CBT principles, and guides users about mindfulness and other emotional well-being practices.

Similarly, Tess by X2AI is an AI-powered chatbot designed to provide psychological assistance. It simulates human-like understanding and communicates in an empathetic manner, suggesting cognitive, mindfulness, and positivity strategies to the users based on their emotional state. In the world of apps, Replika is making strides by learning and growing with the users, delivering a personalised experience.

7.5. The Future: Possibilities and Potential

Looking ahead, the growth and expansion of AI-assisted online therapy is promising. The potential implementation scenarios are vast. Counselors and psychologists can use the technology to help manage their caseload and provide immediate assistance to those in crisis. Schools and universities can incorporate AI therapy platforms to help students manage stress and mental health issues. Workplaces can offer AI therapeutic support as part of their wellness programs, combatting the widespread issue of work-related stress.

By continually refining their capabilities to understand, empathize, learn, and provide suitable intervention, AI-equipped therapy platforms are shaping a future where professional mental health support is ubiquitous and accessible to all. This transformative synthesis of technology and emotional support might soon become a common association, bringing AI's warmth and empathy into our daily lives.

In conclusion, AI is gradually taking its place as a warm companion in our journey toward health - physical, mental, and emotional. It is decoding and shaping the future of online therapy, positioning itself as a reliable ally in our pursuit of emotional stability and well-being. The message is clear - AI's function and impact extend beyond its mechanical connotation or technological relevance. It is signalling a new chapter in emotional intelligence, lighting the way towards a more empathetic technological future.

Chapter 8. AI and Mindfulness: Practicing Self-care in the AI-era

The clamoring world around us often tends to overpotentiate our minds, leaving us dizzy in the whirlwind of emotions. Amidst this chaotic blend of emotions, responsibilities, and the bustle of life, practicing self-care often takes the backseat. However, in the advancing era marked by AI technologies, with their daunting, yet intriguing promises of innovation, there exists a silver lining. AI is not just about algorithms, databases, and unimaginable processing abilities, it is about the human touch to technology. The quintessence of AI is its ability to understand, empathize, and elevate the human mind's experience, enhancing our voyage towards mindfulness.

8.1. Understanding AI and Its Intersectionality with Mindfulness

AI has been capacitated to understand the complex weavings of human emotion, thus making it an efficient tool for promoting mindfulness, which is essentially about being in the present and acknowledging emotions without judgment. AI algorithms can monitor our patterns and subtly guide us to acknowledge when our thoughts are drifting into the realm of maladaptive rumination or unnecessary worry.

Various applications have been designed which prompt mindfulness practices, such as breath tracking, mindful eating, and meditation, all powered by AI's predictive analytics and data patterns. It promotes a culture of self-reflection and self-care, thereby laying the foundation for emotional well-being.

AI-assisted technologies are not in any sense substitutes for professional help. Instead, they function as convenient tools to remind individuals to move away from stressors and afford some moments of self-care while traversing the rich tapestry of daily life.

8.2. Unveiling AI-Powered Mindfulness Applications

Mindfulness mobile applications powered by AI have already begun to invade the market, replete with tools to combat stress and promote mental health. These AI-driven apps offer various features like personalized mindfulness routines, voice-guided meditations, mood tracking and feedback, cognitive behavioral therapy exercises, and guided relaxation techniques, among others.

Mindfulness AI apps are capable of analyzing your emotional state through voice analysis and patterns in your interactions. This enables them to offer resources exactly when you need them the most, thus ensuring a truly personalized self-care experience.

8.3. Nurturing Mental Well-being through AI

Due to the sophistication of AI algorithms, applications can now track and analyze the nuances of our sleep, diet, mood, behavior, and exercise patterns. These are intrinsic components of mental well-being, and AI intervention in these areas simplifies the process of mental health tracking.

Furthermore, AI can detect early signs of stress, anxiety, depression, and other mental health conditions. Early detection is crucial in managing mental health, and AI plays a crucial role in providing early intervention. Such tools make mental health care more accessible to users and promote an open culture of mental health discussion and self-care routine.

The sophisticated AI works diligently to enrich your overall well-being by gently pulling you back to the present, prompting you to pause, breathe, and immerse in the moment. Notable, isn't it? AI, essentially an epitome of technological advancement, urging you to celebrate simplicity, peace, and mindfulness!

8.4. Conclusion: Embracing AI for Mindful Living

AI, paradoxically, brings us closer to our quotidian existence by promising an enhanced human experience. It amplifies our ability to cultivate mindfulness by providing immediate resources, context-specific advice, and consistent support. Despite being an edifice of intricate technology, AI exemplifies barefoot living - acknowledging emotions, reaching out and taking care of mental health, relishing the present moment, and lavishing love on oneself.

In a world characterized by complexities, AI simplifies the journey towards mindfulness, striking a perfect balance between progress and peaceful existence. The inexhaustible potential of AI encourages and enables each one of us to take a mindful leap towards self-care and emotional well-being in this AI-era.

Basking in the realm of technology, let us learn to stumble, pause, breathe, heal, and appreciate. It is time to unfurl the power of AI, to venture into the journey of mindfulness, to conduce a living that is as captivating as a ballad, yet as simple as a lullaby. As we navigate the uncharted seas of the future, let self-care and mindfulness be our steadfast anchors, strengthened further by the wind called Artificial Intelligence. Technology can indeed be warm and human; all that's left is for us to embrace it with open hearts and mindful minds.

Chapter 9. Case Studies: Success Stories of AI in Mental Wellness

With the emergence of AI, the landscape of mental health has been irreversibly altered. While the narratives of successful AI integration in the arena of mental wellness are vast and varied, we have picked out significant studies that underscore the potential and promise that this technology brings.

9.1. AI in Therapy: Wysa

One such success story that stands out is a mobile application called 'Wysa'. Powered by AI, Wysa is a smart chatbot serving as an emotional wellness coach. It was developed in response to the growing mental health crisis and the lack of adequate resources. Engineered to offer psychological support, Wysa provides users with self-help techniques, meditations, and cognitive behavioral therapy (CBT).

Complementing its psychological resources, the AI-powered chatbot utilizes machine learning to understand emotional patterns. It can recognize a user's emotional state through their messages, mirroring emotions, and offering empathetic feedback.

Within just a few years of its launch, Wysa has impacted more than 3 million lives across 30 countries. Users have reported consistent improvements in their mood after using the app, showcasing the ability of AI to provide compact, accessible, and effective mental health resources.

9.2. Deep Learning for Depression Detection: Clarifai

In another case, Clarifai, a leading AI company, developed a deep learning model to identify features of depression from images posted on social media platforms. This breakthrough stems from the higher probability of depressed individuals using darker, greyer, and less vibrant colors in their photos. The AI model classified images with an accuracy rate of over 70%, providing invaluable help in detecting potential cases of depression and helping medical professionals reach people who might not have sought help.

The use of AI to detect subtle trends and patterns that allude to mental health issues is a transformative development in preventative mental health care. However, ethical considerations regarding privacy and consent will be paramount in further advancements.

9.3. Virtual Reality Based Therapies: Limbix

In the realm of Virtual Reality (VR), we find real-world applications of AI in improving mental wellness. Limbix, a therapeutics company, uses a combination of VR and AI for exposure therapy – a modality for anxiety disorders where patients are gradually exposed to their fears or anxiety triggers in a safe setting.

With a VR headset, patients can experience simulations close to their real-life scenarios. AI serves to customize these scenarios to mimic patients' specific triggers. Early users of Limbix's system have reported significant reductions in anxiety levels and improved coping mechanisms.

Speaking volumes about the potential we can harness from this technology, such therapies give a glimpse of the future where AI can curate personalized mental health therapies.

9.4. Mood-Predictive Wearables: Empatica

We also have AI integrated wearable technology like Empatica's Embrace2, which predicts mood changes in psychologically sensitive individuals. This device, worn on human wrists, captures bio-signals that predict a user's emotional state. Recognizing the physiological associations with mental states, AI can alert users to impending mood shifts, helping them take proactive steps for stabilizing their emotional well-being.

In people prone to epileptic seizures, caregivers can receive codes from Embrace2 beforehand, enabling pre-emptive action. Thus, AI serves to not only manage existing health issues but curtail potential ones.

9.5. Mental Fitness AI Coach: Mindstrong

Lastly, we look at Mindstrong – a mental fitness app that warrants special mention. It uses AI to identify digital biomarkers from smartphone usage patterns, thereby predicting a user's mental cognitive functionality. Whether it's the speed of typing or the pattern of scrolling, Mindstrong's AI can intelligently map mental health index correlatives. With the user's permission, the app can also alert mental healthcare professionals in emergency mental health crises.

Each success story offers a unique angle on the potential that AI has to revolutionize mental health transformatively. AI isn't just about providing solutions; instead, it's carving new avenues, empowering individuals on their journey towards mental wellness, and filling the existential gaps in the existing mental health landscape. The possibilities are vast, affirming that we are just at the dawn of the AI and mental wellness merger, with the promise of a brighter, healthier future ahead.

Chapter 10. Challenges and Ethical Considerations in AI for Emotional Well-being

Emotional well-being is an intricate tapestry woven with unique threads of experiences, emotions, and an individual's capacity to manage them. The concept of utilizing Artificial Intelligence (AI) to nurture and foster emotional well-being through diverse practical applications isn't without its share of challenges and ethical considerations. Let's delve into evaluating these critical facets of incorporating AI within mental health support mechanisms.

10.1. Understanding the Challenges

Encompassing powerful processing abilities and the knack to mimic human thought process and emotions, AI does undeniably hold immense promise for supporting emotional well-being. However, the pathway leading to these benefits is strewn with obstacles that need to be addressed before realizing AI's full potential in this domain.

1. **Data privacy and security**: The confidentiality of the client's data is pivotal in any healthcare application, including mental health. As AI relies heavily on data for efficient functioning, maintaining privacy and data security becomes a top priority. There are potential risks of data breaches when incorporating AI platforms into therapeutic applications, and these risks can undermine the trust between users and the AI application.

2. **Quality of collected data**: To make accurate predictions, AI needs high-quality, relevant data. However, collecting large diverse datasets, representing varied demographics and emotional states, becomes a challenge. Besides, people might unintentionally report inaccurately about their feelings or

experiences, leading to 'noisy' data that can impede AI's performance.

3. **Algorithmic Bias**: Algorithms learn from the data they are fed. If the data is biased, the AI could reflect these biases in its predictions and responses, leading to potential harm or misrepresentation, especially for marginalized communities.

4. **Dependency**: While AI can provide support and assistance, there's a risk of over-reliance or dependency on these tools. This could in turn limit human interactions which are vital for emotional growth and understanding.

5. **Lack of Personalization**: Emotions are highly individualistic and subjective experiences. If the AI systems are not tailored to cater to the unique emotional needs of each individual, the efficacy of the treatment might be compromised.

10.2. The Ethical Conundrum

In tandem with the technical challenges mentioned above, integrating AI into emotional health applications also stirs an array of ethical concerns.

1. **Informed Consent**: Often, users are not fully aware of how their data is collected, used, and stored by AI platforms. The notion of informed consent gets skewed in such scenarios, leading to ethical disputes.

2. **Accuracy and reliability**: AI systems may misinterpret emotional signals leading to inaccurate assessments. The ethical implication here is the potential harm this misinterpretation can cause, especially, for instance, when diagnosing mental health conditions or guiding therapeutic interventions.

3. **Accountability**: In scenarios where AI gives incorrect advice or misdiagnoses a condition, there's an ethical question concerning who should be held accountable - the provider, the developer of

the AI, or the AI itself?

4. **Dehumanization of care**: Emotional well-being is often rooted in interpersonal connections and empathy. Relying too heavily on AI might strip the human touch from mental health care, adding a further layer of complication to the ethical muddle.

5. **Accessibility and Equality**: AI applications might be inaccessible to those who cannot afford them, leading to inequality in mental health resources distribution and further deepening the existing digital divide.

Each of the challenges and ethical issues highlighted above merits substantial attention in discussions, research, and policy formulation for AI's use in emotional well-being. As we continue to navigate through the realm of AI, proliferating its use in diverse areas, it is crucial that we tread carefully, balancing the potential advantages and pitfalls competently. Doing so will help ensure that AI functions as a powerful tool in promoting emotional well-being rather than becoming a detrimental force.

Chapter 11. Embracing the Future: The Road Ahead for AI in Mental Health Support

AI, mental health, and their symbiosis have emerged as a focus of interest in the recent years due to growing incidence of mental health ailments and our limited human resources to grapple with them. Let's look ahead and envision the inroads AI promises to make in the mental health sphere, embarking on a journey from awareness to action.

11.1. Grasping the Current Landscape

Our world, for the most part, remains largely unaware of the significant role emotions play in our everyday lives. However, increasing conversations around mental health have challenged this status quo and brought wellbeing initiatives to the forefront. Leveraging AI in this transformative period presents a golden opportunity, promising widespread benefits.

AI's role in mental health support lies in its ability to comprehensively assist on three fronts: detection, intervention, and prevention. The current landscape is focused on its application in early detection, where machine learning algorithms are trained to accurately detect different variations of emotional states, moods and potential mental health conditions. AI's potential for early detection is substantial, promising to capture more complex, nuanced emotional states than traditional psychological diagnostics.

This early detection capability of AI is currently paired with digital interventions such as AI-based therapy chatbots, virtual reality therapy, and wearable mood trackers. These applications are just the beginning, and the landscape is still blooming with opportunities for AI technology's growth and prevalence in mental health support.

11.2. Emerging AI Innovations and Approaches

AI research has always lived on the cutting edge of innovation. Mental health is no exception, as groundbreaking solutions have surfaced to give us a glimpse into what the future of mental healthcare could look like. AI's potential to improve the accessibility, immediacy, and personalization of mental health support is paramount.

AI's ability to continuously learn and adapt makes it perfect for designing interventions that evolve with individual users. For instance, chatbots designed to provide cognitive behavioral therapy (CBT) can adapt their strategies over time, providing patients with more personalized support. Meanwhile, AI innovations in teletherapy have made therapy accessible to individuals who are unable or uncomfortable attending therapy in person.

Similarly, the future may see a rise in AI-driven "empathy analytics." These tools will leverage AI's deep learning capabilities to interpret human emotion accurately. AI could then create responsive, emotionally aware interventions – a significant leap in mental healthcare.

11.3. The Power of Predictive Analytics

Predictive analytics, a branch of advanced analytics, uses historical data, ML algorithms and statistical techniques to predict future outcomes. The potential of predictive analytics in mental health is enormous. Using AI to analyze personal and environmental data, predictive models could anticipate mental health crises before they happen.

Imagine a wearable device that not only tracks heart rate but uses this data in conjunction with other parameters like sleep patterns, physical activity, and social interactions to proactively recognize emotional distress or potential depressive episodes. AI could then trigger immediate interventions or alert the user or their support system. The implications on this front are profound, making way for proactive mental healthcare.

11.4. AI for Mental Health in a Post-Pandemic World

The pandemic has significantly amplified the need for innovative solutions to mental health support. Widespread feelings of isolation, fear, and distress have triggered a global mental health crisis and highlighted the inadequacy of current support systems.

The integration of AI in mental health support systems will allow us to expand our reach and scale without compromising on the quality of support. We could provide continuous care, with AI picking up on patterns that even the most experienced psychologists might miss. Moreover, given the broad accessibility of AI, individuals in remote locations or those unable or unwilling to seek in-person assistance will have confidential, personalized, and immediate support available.

11.5. Philosophical Considerations and Ethical Boundaries

In spite of its potential, AI's integration in mental health also brings up important ethical and philosophical considerations. From concerns about data privacy and consent to philosophical questions about the nature of empathy and emotional connection, these discussions are vital to AI's progress.

While AI tools can collect extensive personal data, they must be designed to protect and respect user privacy. Data collected should only be used with the user's explicit consent and for the specific purpose intended. The same privacy standards in place for traditional therapy should apply to all AI-based interventions.

On a philosophical level, some argue that emotional support requires empathy – a trait AI inherently lacks. While an AI system can be trained to mimic empathetic responses, it's unable to truly understand and experience human emotions. It's critical to preserve the human factor in mental health solutions. AI should complement, not replace, human therapists.

Looking ahead, there is no doubt that a blend of AI technology and human understanding could be instrumental in fostering our emotional well-being. As we cautiously navigate the philosophical and ethical complexities, we must not lose sight of the overarching goal of AI's integration in mental health - to enhance and uplift the human experience. There will bumpy pathways, yes, but for every stumbling block, there are a thousand asteroids of hope! AI's promise for our emotional wellbeing is exactly that - a lustrous asteroid radiating the hope of a harmonious symbiosis of man and machine.